not a guide to
Shrewsbury

Samantha Lyon

The History Press

First published in 2012

The History Press
The Mill, Brimscombe Port
Stroud, Gloucestershire, GL5 2QG
www.thehistorypress.co.uk

British Library Cataloguing in Publication Data.
A catalogue record for this book is available from the British Library.

ISBN 978 0 7524 7120 4

Typesetting and origination by The History Press
Printed in Great Britain

Coat of Arms

The Shrewsbury coat of arms traditionally depicts three 'loggerheads' (leopard heads), with the motto *Floreat Salopia* underneath. This Latin phrase translates as 'May Shrewsbury flourish'.

*

A separate design for the Shrewsbury Coat of Arms exists, which depicts three lions in place of the leopards. This confusion may be due to the early English heralds, who often confused leopards with lions.

*

In 1896 Shropshire County Council established arms with loggerheads, but in 1975 the now abolished Shrewsbury and Atcham Borough Council established the alternative coat of arms.

Contents

Pronunciation and Definition

Pronounced /ʃruːzbri/ or /ʃroʊzbri/.
This difference in pronunciation has always been highly debated amongst the locals.

Shrewsbury was known to the Anglo-Saxons as Scrobbesbyrig, which had a few meanings (the most notable of which being 'the town of the bushes'). Its Welsh name, Amwythig, means 'fortified place', but Shrewsbury is known to most as 'the town of flowers'.

Grid Reference

Shrewsbury High Street: 52° 42' 23.63" N, 2° 45' 4.62" W

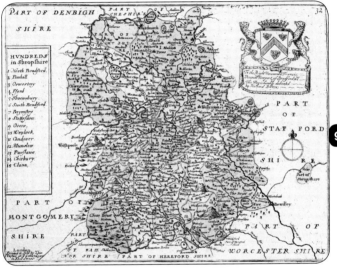

On the Map

First appearance on a map

The oldest known map of Shrewsbury is the Burghley map of around 1575, commissioned by Lord Burghley at a time of rapid change in Shrewsbury.

Position on a UK map

See opposite.

Street Names

Shrewsbury has a mixture of amusing and historical street names, many of which date back to medieval times. Below are some examples:

Dogpole – Unusual as this name might seem, this is one example that has survived the centuries, along with Grope Lane, Gullet Passage and Bear Steps.

Grope Lane – This is probably the best known 'shut' in Shrewsbury. A few theories exist as to how it got its name. The narrow alleyway is surrounded by overhanging buildings, meaning that at night it can be incredibly dark. Some people believe this street was given its name because pedestrians had to grope their way through the alleyway. Another popular (and more likely) theory is that the name refers to the activities that took place there after dark. In fact, many medieval towns had Grope Lanes, though most have been renamed.

Gullet Passage – 'Gullet' comes from the old English word *golate*, meaning stream. This street gets its name from an old stream that used to run from the Square to the River Severn.

Pengwern Road – Shrewsbury was known to the ancient Britons as Pengwern, which is how this name came about.

Mary Webb Road – This was named after local novelist and poet Mary Webb (1881-1927).

Fish Street – This is possibly the most photographed street in the town, which is understandable given the medieval buildings and cobbled road. It is another example of a centuries-old street name.

Butcher Row – The meaning of this street is clearly evident. This is where the medieval butchers would trade, but back in the day it would have been best to avoid this street, with all manner of meaty cast-offs littering its floor.

Suburbs and Wards

Shrewsbury has a number of suburbs and wards which have become progressively more important as the town expands and develops. Places like Bayston Hill are now considered suburbs of Shrewsbury but maintain their own parish council. Below is a list of some Shrewsbury suburbs.

Abbey Foregate – Located near the English Bridge, this suburb is home to a famous Shrewsbury church known as 'The Abbey', which was founded in 1083 by the first Earl of Shrewsbury, Roger de Montgomery.

Bangley – This suburb is named after a brook that flows through to the Severn at Chester Street.

Copthorne – This is a residential suburb which includes several public houses, two schools, a tennis club and a shopping centre.

Coton Hill – This suburb is home to the unusually named 'Pig Trough' passage. Every year the Shropshire and West Midlands Show is held just outside Coton Hill on the Shropshire Agricultural Showground. An interesting note for pub-goers: this suburb has an unusual amount of public houses, all in very close proximity. These include the Severn Apprentice and the Woody (more formally known as the Woodman Inn).

Ditherington – This ward is home to the oldest iron-framed building in the world, which is well known as 'the grandfather of skyscrapers'. The Grade I listed building was designed by William Strutt in 1797.

Frankwell – There are several theories as to how this suburb got its name. One suggestion is that it originated from 'Frankville', which means a town of free trade – which would be fitting, as it is located close to the Severn and developed as a port and trading location. Located just outside the town centre, Frankwell is one of Shrewsbury's oldest suburbs and is sometimes known by its nickname, 'Little Borough'.

Harlescott – This is an extremely industrial area. Each Sunday, an open-air market, where you can buy anything from clothing to fresh meat, is held near the local Tesco.

Sundorne – Sundorne, which is located north of Shrewsbury town centre, is well equipped with its own library, community centre and sports centre. It is also home to AFC Sundorne. This ward suffers from the occasional identity crisis, with some of the inhabitants and businesses referring to it as 'Harlescott', a neighbouring suburb. In fact, the local school changed its name from Harlescott School to Sundorne School to avoid confusion.

Distance From...

Place	Miles	Km
Sydney	10,621	17,092
Brussels	329	530
Centre of the Earth	3,975	6,397
Death Valley	5,140	8,271
Eiffel Tower	459	739
Frankfurt	523	843
Guernsey	4,000	6,438
Hong Kong	6,034	9,710
Dubai	3,527	5,676
Jerusalem	2,381	3,831
Ankara	2,399	3,861
London Eye	140	225
Cerne Abbas Giant	210	188
Stonehenge	117	188
Osaka	5,904	9,501
Mecca	3,119	5,019
Queenstown	11,792	18,975
Reykjavik	1,045	1,681
The Bullring	40	64
Giant's Causeway	341	549
Zutphen	379	610
Vatican City	1,029	1,656
Singapore	6,842	11,010
Amsterdam	323	520
Ibiza	975	1,569
Zurich	622	1,000

Twinned Towns

Shrewsbury is twinned with only one town, that being Zutphen in the Netherlands. This twinning was made official in 1977, but an informal arrangement has been in existence since the Second World War. Voluntary Twinning Committees in both cities organise yearly visits for the mayor and town clerk. The Shrewsbury Zutphen Twinning Committee aims to encourage and aid twinning links and exchanges, as well as putting individuals who are interested in twinning in touch with one another.

Like Shrewsbury, Zutphen is an historic town with remarkable buildings. It is a small town, with a population of roughly 51,000.

Shrewsburys Abroad

Location	Population
Shrewsbury, Massachusetts, USA	35,608
Shrewsbury, Missouri, USA	6,644
Shrewsbury, New Jersey, USA	3,809
Shrewsbury, Pennsylvania, USA	3,378
Shrewsbury, Vermont, USA	1,108
Shrewsbury, West Virginia, USA	652
Shrewsbury, Quebec, Canada	0 (it's a ghost town)

Historical Timeline

Mammoths roam
Shrewsbury.

Battle of
Shrewsbury.

Shrewsbury is
covered by the sea;
the Wrekin and
the Long Mynd
begin to form.

Shrewsbury Castle
is founded by
the first Earl of
Shrewsbury, Roger
de Montgomery.

Shrewsbury
Old Market
Hall is built.

**4600-545 million
years ago**

**13,000
years ago**

1070

1403

1590

**200-145 milion
years ago**

901

1083

1552

1719

Earliest written
documentation
of Shrewsbury
being a town.

Shrewsbury
School is built.

The Jurassic period:
dinosaurs wander
Shrewsbury.

Shrewsbury
Abbey founded.

The Quarry is
created.

The Welsh Bridge is built, costing £8,000.

Shrewsbury Town Football Club is founded.

Construction on Theatre Severn begins.

The English Bridge is built, costing £16,000.

On the Origin of Species is published.

Darwin Shopping Centre is built.

| 1774 | 1795 | 1859 | 1886 | 1989 | 2007 |
| 1792 | 1809 | 1881 | 1977 | 2005 | 2009 |

St Chad's church is built.

Mary Webb, novelist and poet, is born.

Shrewsbury is twinned with Zutphen.

The Quantum Leap structure is unveiled in honour of Darwin's bicentenary.

Charles Darwin is born.

The Shrewsbury Flower Show is mentioned in the *Guinness Book of Records* for being the longest-running flower show in the world.

Freak Weather

Although Shrewsbury's weather is usually fair, the town has had one or two instances of unusual weather. One notable month would be August of 1990, when the weather reached an extraordinary 34.9°C. This is the hottest Shrewsbury has ever been. Conversely, in the December of 1981, the temperature plummeted to an unearthly -25.2°C – weather more suited to the South Pole than Britain. Thankfully, the weather doesn't make a habit of plunging so drastically.

Unfortunately, given the fact that Shrewsbury is located within a horseshoe of river, it is very susceptible to flooding. The autumn of 2000 is a prime example and the worst case of flooding in the area for over fifty years. The town was flooded three times in the space of six weeks, and Frankwell was particularly affected. The Frankwell flood defences were completed in 2003, meaning that although the Severn has flooded since, the town hasn't been so severely affected. The winter of 2007 is an exception: flooding rendered some of the town car parks unusable, thereby reducing trade in Shrewsbury in the run-up to Christmas.

Fun Facts

The River Severn is thought to have derived from the Celtic *Sabrinn-â*. This word then became 'Sabrina' to the Romans. In mythology, the nymph Sabrina drowned in the Severn.

Mardol, a street that has a huge number of interesting buildings, means 'Devil's Boundary' or 'the Devil's End'.

Shrewsbury School was one of the original nine Clarendon Schools, which include Eton and Rugby.

The River Severn is Britain's most dangerous river, having claimed many lives over the years – around 300 is the usual estimate.

The oldest building in the world to house a McDonald's is located in Shrewsbury. One of the exterior walls can be dated back to the thirteenth century.

The Shrewsbury Regatta, organised by Pengwern Boat Club, is one of the oldest amateur rowing events in the UK.

Carol Ewels, local author, wrote two children's books about 'Jack the Cat' which were set in Shrewsbury.

St Mary's spire is the third tallest in England.

A Day in Shrewsbury

0800 – Morning Prayer at St Chad's.

0900 – Shops open.

1000 – Shrewsbury Museum and Art Gallery opens to the public.

1030 – Shropshire Regimental Museum opens.

1100 – The *Sabrina* boat begins its hourly, 40 minute sail of the River Severn loop.

1200 – Food is served at the Lion Hotel.

1430 – Walking tours of Shrewsbury begin.

1500 – Schools let out.

1530 – Movies start playing at the cinema.

1600 – People can be found enjoying afternoon tea in the Prince Rupert Hotel.

1700 – Shops close.

1800 – Curry houses open.

2000 – Performances are underway at Theatre Severn.

2300 – Nightclubs are in full swing.

How Many Times...

52

The number of times a year the *Shrewsbury Chronicle* is published (it has been published weekly since the first edition, in 1772).

6

The number of times a year Shrewsbury hosts a show or festival.

1,092

The number of times a year that St Chad's holds a service.

31

The number of times a year the shops provide late-night shopping.

269

The number of times a year the Theatre Severn stages a performance.

12

The number of times a year Shrewsbury Farmers' Market is held in the town square.

312

The number of times a year a competitive squad trains at the Pengwern boat club.

52

The number of times a year the Shrewsbury Morris Dancers rehearse.

1,210

The number of times a year a dog gets rehomed by Shrewsbury's Dogs Trust.

1.6 million

The number of times a year a passenger enters or exits Shrewsbury train station.

Demographics

These figures were taken from the 2001 Census and are for Shrewsbury and Atcham:

Population:	95,850
Male	47,072
Female	48,780
Single inhabitants	20,752
Married or remarried	41,489
Separated or divorced	8,131
Cohabiting couple households	3,439

Ethnicity:	
White	94,308
Ethnic individuals	1,542

Religion:	
Christian	74,701
Buddhist	196
Hindu	106
Muslim	263
Sikh	63
No religion/religion not stated	20,286

More Demographics

Average household size

2.32

Hold a first degree or equivalent

14,252

Migrants who moved to the area from within the UK

383

Single male parents

226

Owner-occupiers

29,839

Average number of rooms per household

5.79

Number of people who travel to work on a bicycle

2,377

Number of houses that have three or more cars or vans

2,661

Number of unemployed citizens

6,677

Number of people in good (or fairly good) health

87,896

Facts and Statistics

37.8 per cent

The percentage of the population that work in the public administration, education and health sector, making it the largest industry in the town.

133ft

The height of Lord Hill's column, located just outside Shropshire Council, making it the tallest Doric column in the world.

£28 million

The cost of the Theatre Severn.

£249,723

The average detached house price in Shrewsbury.

52,181

The population of Shrewsbury and Atcham in 1901.

£28,000

The amount spent on the sponsorship of the Shrewsbury Flower Show for 2010 and 2011.

6

The room number in the Prince Rupert Hotel that is haunted by the ghost of a jilted bride.

183 per cent

The capacity to which HMP Shrewsbury is filled. It is reportedly the most overcrowded prison in the UK.

£450,000

The original estimated cost of the Quantum Leap structure (unveiled in honour of Darwin's bicentenary).

£1 million

What Quantum Leap ended up costing after alignment problems were fixed.

Famous For...

The Shrewsbury Biscuit – Sometimes referred to as a Shrewsbury cake, this popular dessert that has been around for centuries. Interestingly, the Shrewsbury Biscuit is well-loved in India and is produced in Pune.

Simnel cake – This is another centuries-old recipe for cake, similar to Christmas cake, and is traditionally eaten during the Easter period. Other towns have their own recipes, but over the years the Shrewsbury recipe has proven to be the most popular.

Wool – In the Middle Ages, Shrewsbury was integral in the wool trade. Specifically, Shrewsbury was involved in the finishing of Welsh cloth, which would then be sent to London to sell.

Shropshire Lad – This bitter was first brewed in 1996, 100 years after Housman's poems were published. It is produced by the Wood Brewery and is their best seller.

Lemon Dream – This extremely popular beer is produced by the Salopian Brewery and has won an award at CAMRA West Midlands four years in a row.

The Shrewsbury Flower Show – This event, organised by the Shropshire Horticultural Society, has been held in the Quarry Park every August since 1875. It takes place over two days and attracts thousands of visitors every year.

Scrooge's grave – Shrewsbury was used as part of the set for the 1984 movie *A Christmas Carol*. Lots of the interior and exterior shots were of Shrewsbury, and Ebenezer Scrooge's gravestone is still in St Chad's graveyard.

Charles Robert Darwin – Darwin (1809-1882) was born in Shrewsbury and remains a huge source of pride for the town. His name is lent to the Darwin Shopping Centre, Darwin Street and the modern monument Darwin Gate (to name a few). In 2009, a 40ft sculpture named Quantum Leap was unveiled in tribute of Charles Darwin's bicentenary. Even a local nightclub honours Darwin with its name, Evolution.

The Lion Hotel – This seventeenth-century coaching inn has been part of Shrewsbury's history for 400 years. The luxury accommodation makes it perfect for short weekend breaks, especially as it is so close to the town's shops and cafés. It still has the original ballroom, oak beams and inglenook fireplace. The hotel has been frequented by many famous names, including King William IV, Paganini, Benjamin Disraeli, and Charles Dickens. In fact, Dickens wrote *The Pickwick Papers* during his stay.

Mary Webb – This romantic novelist was born in 1881 in the nearby village of Leighton. Her most well-known novel was arguably *Gone to Earth*, which was made into a film in 1950, directed by Michael Powell.

Infamous For...

The iPad controversy – In July 2011, protesters raved when Shropshire Council spent £12,000 on new iPads for their staff. The timing was particularly bad as the decision to spend thousands coincided with the week that the Grange Day Centre for disabled adults was shut down by the council. On the other hand, the iPads are being introduced in order to switch to paperless meetings, and the council claims that it will save more than £100,000 per year.

The Hanging Judge – George Jeffreys (1645-1689), commonly known as 'The Hanging Judge', attended Shrewsbury School from 1652-1659. Jeffreys sentenced hundreds of men and women to death, sometimes for surprisingly trivial crimes. Although his legal ability is generally undisputed, some say that it was often compromised by his vengeful nature.

Mad Jack – John 'Mad Jack' Mytton came from an old, respected family. He received his full inheritance at a young age, the modern-day equivalent of £4.3 million, as well as an annual income of an amount worth £716,000. It didn't take him long to squander most of it and then get into serious debt. His eccentric behaviour, including tormenting tutors with practical jokes, getting expelled from school and trying to cure his hiccoughs by setting his shirt on fire, earned him the nickname 'Mad Jack'. At one point Mytton decided that he had parliamentary aspirations and so bribed his constituents into voting for him. He reportedly only attended parliament once – for half an hour. To add to his problems, Mytton had a very serious drinking problem and took 2,000 bottles of port with him to Cambridge University. He ended up running away to France to avoid court and prison.

The Shrewsbury rail accident – On 15 October 1907, a train from Manchester derailed into Shrewsbury station, killing eighteen people. The overnight train was reportedly travelling 60mph on a curve that was limited to 10mph. It is believed that the driver fell asleep and was therefore unable to brake in time.

Quantum Leap – Even setting aside the hefty price tag, this structure (known locally as 'slinky') proves controversial. It was constructed to honour Darwin's bicentennial and is meant to represent the DNA double helix. Unfortunately, the beauty of the structure is far from universally appreciated: most people believe that another statue of Darwin would have been more appropriate. The cost of the structure was estimated to be £450,000 in 2009, but in 2011 this price has more than doubled to an incredible £1 million after alignment problems needed to be fixed. This doesn't include the legal fees incurred through a battle with the contractors, which cost a further £115,000.

Theatre Severn – The infamy of this potentially amazing building arises from two things: the materials used and the fact that a crack developed in the stonework just two years after its erection in 2009. This, of course, meant repairs and further costs. The £28 million building has provoked mixed reactions. Some believe it will attract visitors to the area, while others feel that the look and size of the building doesn't suit the medieval town. From the outside, one can see many different materials – including wood, which some locals insist is already looking warped and discoloured.

Literary References

'They hang us now in Shrewsbury jail:
      The whistles blow forlorn,
And trains all night groan on the rail
      To men that die at morn.
There sleeps in Shrewsbury jail to-night,
      Or wakes, as may betide,
A better lad, if things went right,
      Than most that sleep outside.'
A.E. Housman, *The Shropshire Lad*, 1896

'... we have the strangest little rooms, the ceilings of which I can touch with my hand. The windows bulge out over the street, as if they were little stern windows in a ship, and a door opens out of the sitting room onto a little open gallery with plants in it where one leans over a queer old rail and looks all downhill and slantwise at the crookedest old black and yellow houses...'
Charles Dickens, from a letter to his daughter describing his stay in the Lion Hotel, 1858

'... a sumptuous room allotted to me, it was a ballroom of noble proportions lighted by three gorgeous chandeliers... sparking through all their crystal branches and flashing back the soft rays of my tall, waxen lights.'
Thomas De Quincey, describing his stay in the Lion Hotel, *Confessions of an Opium Eater*, 1821

'...This is indeed a beautiful, large, pleasant, populous, and rich town; full of gentry and yet full of trade too; for here too, is a great manufacture, as well of flannel, as also of white broadcloth, which enriches all the country round it... This is really a town of mirth and gallantry, something like Bury in Suffolk, or Durham in the north, but much bigger than either of them, or indeed than both together... Mr Camden calls it a city: Tis at this day, says he, a fine city well-inhabited: But we do not now call it a city, yet 'tis equal to many good cities in England, and superior to some.'
Daniel Defoe, *A Tour Thro' the Whole Island of Great Britain*, 1724-1727

'A fair town is Shrewsbury –
The world over
You'll hardly find a fairer,
In its fields of clover
and rest-harrow ringed
By hills where curlews call,
And drunken from the heather,
Black bees fall.
Poplars, by Severn,
    Lean hand in hand,
Like golden girls dancing
    In elfland....
Neither bells in the steeple
    Nor books, old and brown,
Can disenchant the people
    In the slumbering town.'
Mary Webb, *The Elf*, 1929

'In this old town I know so well I have dwelt in heaven...'
Mary Webb, *My Own Town*, 1929

'All the people of Shrewsbury,
Playing the old gooseberry, –
They stick up a pole
    In the place that's still called
Wylde Cop
    And they pop
Your grim gory head on the top!'
Thomas Ingoldsby, 'Bloudie Jacke of Shrewsberrie', 1866

In the News

17 December 2007
'Hundreds of motorcyclists gave Father Christmas a hand by taking presents to the children at the Royal Shrewsbury Hospital. They also collected money for various children's charities on their way through the town.'

1 September 2011

'£1.1 million was raised in order to help repair local historic building St Chad's church. The money is needed to repair the tower and the long-term damage to the stonework and bricks. Money is also going to go into refurbishing the organ, making the building weatherproof and upgrading the heating facilities. Another £1.4 million is needed to complete the work.'

23 August 2011
'Ex Shrewsbury Town FC defender Colin Griffin was inducted into Greenhous Meadow's 'Hall of Fame' for being the only player to have started more than 400 League games for the local football club.'

28 September 2010

'In an attempt to reach out to the younger generation and get to grips with the modern day, Shrewsbury Town Council joined Facebook. Some councillors, despite being slightly inexperienced with social networking, believe that joining Facebook will ease communication with the people of Shrewsbury.'

20 January 2009

'A letter came to light, written by Charles Darwin, revealing his frustration with being asked stupid questions from "half the fools throughout Europe". The letter was written in approximately 1879. The guide price for the auction was £1,800 to £2,200.'

23 August 2011

'A £1 million building is set to be built on Priory Road for Shrewsbury Sixth Form College, but a report from Shropshire Council's Archaeology Service claims that medieval human remains could exist under the proposed site. The area under the projected building could have been part of a cemetery for the Augustinian Friary and may date back to 1254. The remains could provide valuable information on population, pathology and disease.'

24 June 2011

'Shrewsbury's three malls, the Pride Hill, Darwin and Riverside shopping centres, will be merged and renamed 'New Riverside' in order to create one big £150 million mall. Under the new plans, a department store will be added and sixty new shops will be created. Work on the malls should be completed by late 2015.'

Letters to the Press

Thanks for helping my son

'I would like through the letters page to send thanks to the very kind gentleman who, on July 24, picked up my very cut, bleeding and bruised son from outside Hadley Learning Community and brought him home together with his bike, which he had put into the back of his car. I cannot express enough thanks to this gentleman. Unfortunately I didn't get a chance to get his name as my son was standing dripping with blood in the kitchen. Might I add that my son is recovering well and luckily needed no stitches. He did give the bike a wide berth for a week or so, though. This act of kindness did restore my faith in society when there is so much doom and gloom around. Again, many thanks to you.'
(E. Phillips, 4 August 2009)

Let there (not) be light

'I was delighted to see Andy Boddington's letter on April 19 about reducing street lighting to give us back the night skies. As an astronomy enthusiast living in the Strettons I particularly support his proposal for a starlight sanctuary in the south Shropshire Hills. Last year, the International Year of Astronomy, the Shropshire Astronomical Society attracted a lot of public interest at two observing sessions at Attingham Hall. Last month a public meeting about astronomy at the National Trust centre in Carding Mill Valley attracted well over 100 people of all ages, and there is a lot of interest in holding local observing evenings.

I hope there will be plenty of public support for our councils in exploring well thought-out, selective reductions in lighting, and better lighting systems than the motorway-style floodlights which disfigure our towns and villages. It's a win-win opportunity in the present economic crisis: lower energy costs, a reduced carbon footprint, and the restoration to our grandchildren of one of nature's most stunning marvels.'
(Rt Revd Michael Bourke, 6 May 2010)

Something very sad about the sale of reference books

'For the past two weeks there's been a sale of books at the reference library at Shrewsbury. It ended on August 26. It featured a wonderful collection of books on a variety of subjects and special interests. This will never be repeated in this town.

Some say that you can obtain anything on the internet; the question being, who feeds the net? Our libraries were stocked by highly skilled librarians and committees who catered for a wide taste. We've lost something very special with this sale.

I've gained some very interesting books. Sad they can't be shared by my fellow Salopians who are looking for a book on a specialist subject in the county library. Today they say we must progress and embrace IT.

I don't know: there's something special in the feel of a book and the joy of finding something you want in those paper pages.'

(John R. Brown, 7 September 2011)

Museums, Art Galleries and Attractions

The Shropshire Regimental Museum – Established in 1985, this museum is located in Shrewsbury Castle. If you have an interest in military collections, the Shropshire Regimental Museum is certainly worth a visit. The museum spans three floors, with its main focus being on the King's Shropshire Light Infantry and the county's artillery.

Gallery SCA – This gallery was established to introduce contemporary art to Shropshire. It contains an exciting mix of both 2D and 3D art and aims to support aspiring artists, including painters, sculptures, jewellers and ceramicists.

Shrewsbury Museum and Art Gallery – This museum holds a modest but fascinating collection that dates back to 12,000 BC. The collections celebrate Shropshire's variety and contain a range of Bronze Age metalwork. Shrewsbury Museum and Art Gallery is the headquarters of Shrewsbury Museums Service.

Coleham Pumping Station – This location would be worth a visit for those with an interest in historical, nineteenth-century sewage pumping stations. The station, built in 1900, resembles a Victorian chapel and houses two steam engines that can be seen running together on select open days.

The Quarry – This 29-acre park, created in 1719, is the location for the Shrewsbury Flower Show. Considering the Severn runs through the park, it is ideal for a walk or a picnic and demonstrates very effectively how Shrewsbury came to be known as the 'Town of Flowers'. The best time to see the Quarry is in the summer months, but even in the winter the park is picturesque, with its ponds and fountains. In the past, the park has helped Shrewsbury win several floral community competitions, including the European Entente Florale, Communities in Bloom, and Britain in Bloom.

Music in Shrewsbury

Shrewsbury has seen the birth of many choirs, and their concerts are always a hit in the town. The churches of Shrewsbury provide amazing acoustics for these groups, and St Chad's, in particular, is a popular forum for all singers. The following are a taste of the musical talent Shrewsbury provides.

Shrewsbury Choral Society – This society was founded in 1941 and at present has over 100 members. They perform approximately four times a year, normally at St Chad's, St Mary's, Shrewsbury Abbey or the Theatre Severn.

Jigsaw Sound – This choir was formed in 2007 by twelve people and now has over eighty members. It is open to all and has become extremely popular, leading to the group Missing Pieces. This allows those wanting to join Jigsaw Sound to practice at their leisure in order to achieve a 'concert-ready' status.

One of Accord – This choir was formed in 1985 and aims to have fun and enjoy music while raising money for a good cause. All you need to join is a passion for music, as this choir doesn't demand that its members have any formal training.

The Shrewsbury Cantata Choir – Founded in 1987, this choir has appeared as the feature choir in three BBC *Songs of Praise* programmes. They rehearse weekly at Shrewsbury School and always welcome new talent.

Buildings

With over 600 listed buildings, Shrewsbury has too many notable buildings to mention in these few pages, but the following are just a few examples of Salopian architecture.

Shrewsbury Castle – Shrewsbury is almost entirely protected by the River Severn, but the red sandstone castle was built in around 1070 as a means to shield the town further. Unfortunately, not much of the original Norman castle remains, with the exception of the gateway. Most of the original castle was destroyed during rebuilding in the fourteenth century. It is now home to the Shropshire Regimental Museum. A pathway leads up the hill from Shrewsbury Castle to Laura's Tower (built in 1790 by Thomas Telford), where you can get an amazing view of the town.

Rowley's House – This is perhaps Shrewsbury's best known timber-framed building. It dates back to around 1590 and is a grade II listed building.

Market Hall – This building was built in the 1960s and is often a sore spot for the locals. Some complain that it looks completely at odds with the rest of the town and resembles a block of flats.

Theatre Severn – This theatre was built in 2009 for £28 million. Construction began in 2007, and the façade makes use of different materials, including brick, wood, steel, and glass. This is an often debated building, provoking a varied mix of reactions.

The Golden Cross – This is reportedly the oldest public house in Shrewsbury, dating back (as an inn) as far as 1428. It has been many things in its time, but it was originally the sacristy of Old St Chad's church and known as the 'Sextry'. It was first recorded as The Golden Cross in 1780, and has been a popular meeting place ever since.

Shrewsbury Library – This building dates back to 1552 and was founded by King Edward VI. In the early 1930s the building was restored, at a cost of £3 million. The library was the site of Shrewsbury School until 1882, and was attended by many famous names, including Judge George Jeffreys, Sir Philip Sidney and Charles Darwin. The statue of Darwin that is situated right in front of the library was erected in 1897, fifteen years after his death.

St Alkmund's church – This church was first founded in 912 by King Alfred's daughter, Ethelfleda. This church collapsed in 1711, and the nave of the current church dates back to 1795. The spire was rebuilt in around 1475.

St Chad's church – It is a bit hard not to be proud of such a beautiful building. Built in 1792, the building is round in shape, which is untraditional for a church, and is well known for its sanctuary window. It replaced an earlier church which collapsed in 1788. The church's motto is: 'Open doors, open hearts, and open minds.'

St Mary's church – This building dates back to 970 and was reportedly founded by King Edgar. It is the largest church in Shrewsbury and was built on the site of an earlier Saxon church. Since 1150, the building has been enlarged and enhanced, and features a varied amount of architectural styles from the twelfth to the nineteenth centuries. The church is famous for its stained glass, especially the glass in the east window of the chancel which depicts the Jesse Tree. If you are a lover of stained glass, this is probably the best church in the country to visit. In addition, the spire of St Mary's is one of the tallest in England.

Old Market Hall – Set in Shrewsbury Square and built in 1596, the Old Market Hall was once used by Shrewsbury drapers and dealers to sell Welsh wool that had been finished in the area. In the 1870s, the upstairs portion of the building was converted into offices and a courthouse, but the place now houses a café and small cinema. Outside, a monthly farmers' market is held, and it is also the location for other fairs. Interestingly, the building has a sundial on the outer back wall – but as the building is now surrounded by taller buildings, sun only lights the dial on summer days.

Shrewsbury Abbey – The abbey was once a Benedictine monastery, founded in 1083 by Roger de Montgomery. Although a lot of the monastery was destroyed in the sixteenth century, today part of the church is still intact. It retains four drum-shaped columns from the Norman church as well as fragments from the shrine of St Winefriede. The First World War memorial below the tower includes Wilfred Owen's name, the famous poet who once lived in Shrewsbury and was killed while serving his country in 1918. The abbey attracts thousands of tourists a year for many reasons, one of which being Edith Pargeter's mystery novels (written under the pen name Ellis Peters), *The Chronicles of Brother Cadfael*, which are set in Shrewsbury Abbey.

The Most...

Most beautiful

St Chad's church. The category of 'most beautiful' has some stiff competition, but what really makes this building so outstanding is its unusual circular nave, the huge double staircase, and it's mix of Ionic, Corinthian and Doric styles.

Most ugly

Market Hall. Although we love the shops that are housed within the Market Hall, the 1960s style building clashes with its surroundings and seems to be at complete odds with the rest of the medieval town.

Most modern

Theatre Severn. The Theatre was built to showcase Shrewsbury's talent and to attract new visitors to the town. Whatever your opinion about its exterior, it is the most modern building in Shrewsbury.

Oldest building

St Mary's church. This church, reputedly founded by King Edgar in the tenth century, attracts countless visitors per year.

Oldest public house

The Golden Cross. This family-owned pub, formerly The Sextry, dates back to 1428. In 1933, two timber-framed archways were discovered and are believed to date back to the time of King Henry III.

Most talked about

Theatre Severn. Whether you can't stand its visage, can't stand the price it came at, or are a firm defender of this building, the Theatre Severn certainly provokes a lot of discussion and lively debate.

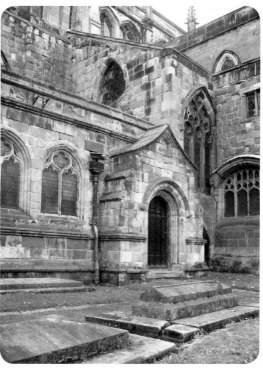

Flora and Fauna of Shrewsbury

The following can be found in and around Shrewsbury, most notably in the Dingle and the Quarry, where the flowers are carefully looked after:

Fumaria purpurea – Purple Rampaging-Fumitory

Saxifraga granulate – Meadow Saxifrage

Cardamine amara – Large Bittercress

Claytonia perfoliata – Spring Beauty

Crocus biflorus – Silvery Crocus

Lythrum salicaria – Purple Loosestrife

Hypericum perforatum – St John's Wort

Scrophularia auriculata – Water Figwort

Rhinanthus minor – Yellow Rattle

Vicia cracca – Tufted Vetch

The River Severn runs through Shrewsbury, giving it a rich wildlife to enjoy. The following birds are often found floating around on the Severn (a good place to view them from would be the Welsh Bridge and the Quarry, by the riverside):

Mergus merganser – Goosander

Tachybaptus ruficollis – Little Grebe

Cygnus olor – Mute Swan

Anas platyrhynchos – Mallard

Chroicocephalus ridibundus – Black Headed Gull

Calopteryx splendens – Banded Demoiselle

The Quarry and the Dingle

The 29-acre park known as the Quarry is a very important and historical part of the town. It is an ideal spot to walk your dog, have a picnic, go for a run or meet with friends. Within these civic gardens is the Dingle, which was once Percy Thrower's personal garden. The high hedges that encapsulate the Dingle give the area a secretive and intimate feel, and the various passages within the Dingle mean you can walk around the whole perimeter and see the range of historical statues, arches and fountains. The Dingle contains an amazing number and variety of flowers, and the good news is that no matter what time of year you visit, there will always be some seasonal colour (although most believe that it looks the best in spring).

When inside the Dingle, make sure to find the following:

The statue of Sabrina – This statue was carved in 1946 by Peter Hollins for the Earl of Bradford. The nymph it depicts is mentioned in John Milton's masque *Comus* (1634)

Entrance arch – This entrance, which is actually a grade II listed building, dates back to the late nineteenth century.

The eagle statue – This sandstone statue, which was originally situated in Kingsland, was moved to the Dingle and unveiled in 1887.

The conduit head – This structure was built in the mid-sixteenth century, with alterations made later on. The estimated year of completion is 1578.

The shoemaker's arbour – Dated from 1679, this semi-circular archway depicts Saint Crispin and Saint Crispian on either side of the coat of arms.

The Dingle fountain – This fountain was cast in 1889 at Coalbrookdale. The cast iron is decorated with shells, leaves and dolphins. The white ceramic statue shows a girl pouring water into a cup.

Home-Grown Companies

Although the largest employer in Shrewsbury is the County Council, which employs over 10,000 people, there are a number of notable businesses in the town. One example is the Salopian Bar, which won the Shrewsbury and West Shropshire Pub of the Year award in 2008, 2009 and 2011. If you are looking for a good pub that provides quality ales, then The Loggerheads might be the pub for you, as it won the CAMRA Pub of the Year award in 2004.

Shrewsbury has a large number of independent shops, but one outstanding shop is Wysteria Lane in Dogpole, which won the Independent Retailer of the Year Award in 2009. Wysteria Lane sells uniquely designed clothes, jewellery and homeware.

The Shropshire Business Awards 2010 (presented by the Shropshire Chamber of Commerce) named Severnside Housing, a not-for-profit company, the best employer in the area, while Dyke Yaxley, a chartered accountants, won an award for best customer service.

Job Sectors

The total figure for jobs held in Shrewsbury and Atcham is 47,100. The breakdown is as follows:

Public admin, education and health

37.8 per cent

Distribution, hotels and restaurants

25.2 per cent

Finance, IT, other business activities

12.6 per cent

Tourism-related

7.7 per cent

Manufacturing

6.8 per cent

Transport and communications

4.8 per cent

Construction

4.7 per cent

The information above was acquired from the ONS annual business inquiry employee analysis, 2008.

Bridges

'High the Vanes of Shrewsbury gleam,
Islanded in Severn stream;
The bridges from the steepled crest,
Cross the water east and west.'
A.E. Housman

The town has many bridges, nine in total, which cross the River Severn and the Rea Brook. It is not every town that can claim that a number of their bridges are actually listed buildings. Being almost surrounded by water, bridges are important to Shrewsbury, and listed below are the five best loved:

Welsh Bridge – This is a Grade II listed building and was built in the 1790s to replace the older St George's Bridge. It was designed by John Tilley and John Carline and is made of Grinshill sandstone.

Porthill Bridge – A pedestrian bridge, built in 1922. It is a suspension bridge, and you can feel obvious vibrations whenever you walk across it.

Kingsland Bridge – A privately owned toll bridge and another Grade II listed building, built in 1881.

English Bridge – The original bridge is known historically as Stone Bridge. This newer bridge was built in 1926 to replace the older one. It is twice as wide as the first, but the original masonry of John Gwynn's 1774 design was used in the rebuild. It is currently listed as a Grade II building.

Shrewsbury railway station – The station is partly built over the river and is listed as a Grade II building.

Born in Shrewsbury

Thomas Parr (1483-1635) – Known as Old Tom Parr, he allegedly lived for 152 years. He is said to have had an affair at 100 and remarried at 122, after the death of his first wife. There are doubts about his age, and some think that he was confused with his grandfather, the father of Henry VIII's wife, Catherine Parr.

Thomas Minton (1765-1836) – The founder of Thomas Minton & Sons in Stoke-on-Trent, Thomas is said to have invented the willow pattern.

John Mytton (1796-1834) – Known as 'Mad Jack', Mytton famously drank his way through his inheritance and fled to France to escape debt collectors.

Charles Darwin (1809-1882) – The famous naturalist.

Mary Webb (1881-1927) – A novelist and poet born in a village southeast of Shrewsbury.

Sandy Lyle (1958-) – This top British golfer won two championships in his time and was once a resident professional at Hawkstone Park, Market Drayton.

Joe Hart (1987-) – This footballer made his debut in 2010 and is already recognised as England's first choice goalkeeper.

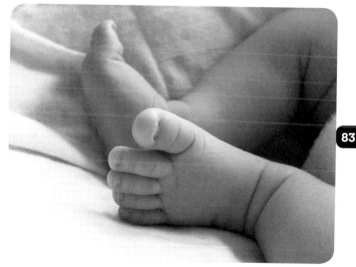

Educated in Shrewsbury

Sir Philip Sidney (1554-1586) – This poet and soldier wrote *Astrophel and Stella* and *The Defence of Poesy*. Attended Shrewsbury School.

Judge George Jeffreys (1648-1689) – Known as 'The Hanging Judge'. Attended Shrewsbury School.

Wilfred Owen (1893-1918) – This famous poet is best known for his war poem *Dulce et Decorum Est*. Attended the Wakeman School, which was known then as Shrewsbury Technical School.

Michael Heseltine (1933-) – A Conservative politician who was an important figure in Margaret Thatcher's and John Major's governments. Educated in Shrewsbury School.

William George Rushton (1937-1996) – Co-founded the *Private Eye* magazine. Attended Shrewsbury School.

Christopher Timothy (1940-) – Welsh actor best known in his role as James Herriot in *All Creatures Great and Small*. Attended Priory Grammar School.

Michael Palin (1943-) – A comedian best known for his travel documentaries and being part of the Monty Python group. Educated in Shrewsbury School.

Flood Alleviation

Shrewsbury's position in a loop of the River Severn makes it extremely susceptible to flooding. Notable examples were the floods that occurred in 1795, when the water reached two metres in Frankwell, and the 2000 floods, the worst flooding in fifty years. The town was badly flooded three times in six weeks: the water reached Shrewsbury Abbey, and more than 200 homes were flooded.

It was the floods in the fall of 2000 that prompted the implementation of flood barriers. Various flood alleviation schemes have been proposed for the town since the 1950s, and in the early 1990s a proposal was rejected because it was believed that the floodwalls would detract from the beauty of the town. These demountable barriers are a happy compromise, as they can be erected whenever there is a risk of flooding. The height of these barriers can be altered depending on the severity of the flood. They are also designed to be erected progressively, meaning that they are put up in a particular sequence, and if flooding is expected soon only the demountable barriers essential to stop flooding will be used. The flood defence scheme focused on the Frankwell area after a feasibility study identified it as the most at risk of flooding.

The plans were put into effect in 2002, and since the implementation of the barriers the town has been mostly safe from flooding. There are rare exceptions (such as in 2007) when the main car park and the houses in New Street were affected.

Shrewsbury Tours

For a taste of Shrewsbury, the Shrewsbury Town Walking Tour is a fantastic introduction to the town. The tour will guide you through the maze of medieval shuts and show off the best-known buildings in the town. The tour will last around two hours and is arranged by the Shrewsbury Visitor Information Centre.

Shrewsbury's own town crier, Martin Wood, offers a few informative tours. The first is a general historical tour of the town, which also lasts approximately two hours. The second is a tour entitled 'Terrible Tudors', which introduces the Tudor houses of Shrewsbury as well as little tidbits about the town. The third is a tour entitled 'Haunted Shrewsbury', which takes place at night to give you a heightened chance of seeing an apparition or ghost.

Finally, a relaxing and leisurely tour is given aboard the *Sabrina*, Shrewsbury's passenger boat, which sails around the Severn loop. There is full commentary aboard, as well as tea, coffee, soft drinks, a licensed bar and snacks. Depending on what day of the week it is, you can see the town in entirely different lights, as the boat offers a Darwin Cruise and a Ghost Cruise, as well as cruises themed with music such as blues and jazz. On specific days, you can experience a Gourmet Fish and Chip cruise, a Mexican Cruise and a Curry Cruise.

Criminals and their Crimes

The Shrewsbury Two – Desmond Warren and the now well-known actor Ricky Tomlinson were arrested for conspiracy after picketing in Shrewsbury during the 1972 building workers' strike. Their imprisonment was greeted with protests and marches, and Tomlinson and Warren protested themselves by refusing to do prison work and wearing nothing but blankets. Warren maintained their innocence for decades, claiming they were simply scapegoats of the system and victims of a political conspiracy.

Ann Harris – In 1828, Ann Harris became the last woman to be executed in public in Shrewsbury. Harris' son, Thomas Ellson, had been implicated in the crime of sheep-stealing, a capital offence at the time. In an attempt to save her son, Harris bribed three men to kill the chief witness in the trial. Without this pivotal witness, the case against Ellson was dropped. However, at a later time – when faced with another charge of animal theft – Ellson cracked and told the authorities where to find the body in order to save himself. Harris was found guilty as an accessory to murder and was sentenced to death by hanging at the Shrewsbury gallows. The role she played in this infamous murder inspired Sir Arthur Conan Doyle's factual piece entitled *The Bravoes of Market Drayton*.

Lawrence Curtis, Patrick Donnelly and Edward Donnelly
– When Sir Robert Peel was in power, various bills were introduced in order to reduce the number of capital crimes, meaning that robbery and arson were no longer punishable by death. The last hangings for robbery took place in Shrewsbury on the 13 August 1836, when Curtis and the Donnelly brothers were hanged.

George Riley – In 1961, Riley became the last man to be hanged at the Dana jail in Shrewsbury. The 21-year-old was found guilty of murdering his neighbour, a 62-year-old widow. There is a chance that this may well have been a horrible miscarriage of justice and that the confession Riley eventually signed wasn't entirely truthful. Riley claimed that his motive for breaking in was theft – even though it transpired that nothing had been taken from her house. Unfortunately, because theft was the motive of the crime, capital punishment was unavoidable under the 1957 Homicide Act. The prisoners of Shrewsbury protested Riley's execution, whistling and chanting for Riley to be freed.

Ghosts and the Unexplained

If you fancy a ghost hunt while you're in the area, keep an eye out for the following spectres:

Mrs Foxhall – The Dingle is meant to be haunted by a woman called Mrs Foxhall, who was burned alive in this very location in 1647 for poisoning her husband.

The milkmaid of Raven Meadows – Raven Meadows is allegedly haunted by a milkmaid, who was accused of adding water to the milk. She walks around and repeats the following rhyme: 'Weight and measure sold I ever, milk and water sold I never.'

The ghosts of Rowley's House – This famous seventeenth-century building is host to two ghosts: one woman and one man. They are both in period costume, and the woman is sometimes seen resting on a bed upstairs. People who have seen the ghosts claim that the man tends to ignore the woman, leading to jokes about a lovers' tiff.

Bloudie Jack – Bloudie Jack haunts the castle grounds. He was once the castle's keeper during the twelfth century and is believed to have killed at least nine young women in his time. After killing them he would drag them across the grounds to the castle. His crimes were eventually discovered, and he was hanged, drawn and quartered.

The cupboard in the Nag's Head – This is one of the most well-known haunted pubs in the country. In its time, the pub has seen three suicides, and legend has it that the deceased each went mad and took their own lives after seeing a picture of a prophet on the inside of a cupboard door. The cupboard is now permanently locked.

The Grey Lady – The Lion Hotel is said to be haunted by an elderly woman who lingers between the powder room and the Adam Ballroom. She has also been seen on the balcony, and many believe that she is sticking around because she is waiting for someone.

The ghosts of the Prince Rupert – The Prince Rupert is said to be haunted by two ghosts, both jilted lovers. The first, a bride-to-be, hanged herself in room six, and the second, who killed himself after his best friend ran off with his fiancée, died in room seven.

Best Bits

Although there's much to love about Shrewsbury, the general consensus seems to be that the following are the best loved (in no particular order):

Shrewsbury Town FC – Here in Shrewsbury, we are extremely loyal to our local football club.

The Dingle – We love it for being an amazing place to go for a walk or to enjoy lunch.

The timber-framed buildings – These buildings make you feel surrounded by history.

The flowers – They're everywhere and it's refreshing to see so much colour, even in winter.

Darwin and Pride Hill Shopping Malls – We love the history of our town, but we would probably go crazy without some modernity! We're extremely grateful for these shops.

Worst Bits

Shrewsbury Bus Depot – Strangely enough, people really seem to dislike the bus station in Shrewsbury, and not only because of its appearance. A lot of people complain that it has become a popular hang-out spot for underage drinkers, making it extremely uninviting to everyone else.

Theatre Severn – Theatre Severn remains a hot topic of conversation, with most claiming it detracts from the beauty of the town.

Lack of recreation – According to an article in the *Shropshire Star* in 2010, the people of Shrewsbury would love an ice-skating rink and a drive-in cinema!

Lack of public transport to outlying villages – Over the past few years, the number of busses to Shrewsbury's outlying villages has decreased significantly, much to the annoyance of those who rely on public transport to get to work or to do their shopping.

No direct train to London – Since the demise of the Wrexham and Shropshire service, where you could hop on at Shrewsbury and off at Marylebone station, the people of Shrewsbury have to do a lot more planning to get to the country's capital.

Must-See Monuments and Statues

Lord Hill's Column – Unveiled in 1816, this Doric column commemorates the famous war general Lord Rowland Hill. Its diameter is 2ft wider than Nelson's Column, and it is 13ft higher.

Clive of India – Erected in 1860. This statue was built to honour Robert Clive, who was once MP for Shrewsbury. It is displayed on top of a column and the foundations of the statue stretch 12ft into the earth to support its weight.

Darwin's Statue – Designed by H. Montford and unveiled in 1894, this statue is located just in front of Shrewsbury Library, which was once the school Darwin attended.

Saint Michael – Designed by Allan Gairdner Wyon and unveiled in 1923, this statue of the Archangel Saint Michael was erected in memory of the men and women of Shropshire who died in the First and Second World Wars. Saint Michael stands under a canopy in the Quarry.

Darwin Gate – Designed by Renn & Thacker and unveiled in 2004, this three-column sculpture is made out of sandstone, glass, copper, steel and bronze. It was inspired by certain features of St Mary's church and is made with the same sandstone. The sculpture also makes use of the 'parallax phenomenon', and the three separate columns appear as one single structure when seen from a particular angle. This unified structure resembles a church window.

Quantum Leap – Designed by Pearce & Lal and unveiled in 2009, this sculpture represents Darwin's innovative scientific ideas. It stands 12 metres high and weighs more than 100 tonnes.

Salopian Slang

Thanks to Shrewsbury School, the town has a number of interesting colloquialisms. Below are a few of the best:

Grot – sweets.

Grot shop – This refers to the school's tuck shop. However, if you have 'heard something in the grot shop', this suggests that what was heard was untrue.

I smell a boosh/waff! – I don't believe it!

Booshy Pete – A nickname for an infamous teacher, remembered for his unbelievable stories. One such tale involved him being lost in the Sahara Desert with a broken-down jeep. Upon opening the doors, Booshy Pete claimed, the wind blew him back to civilisation.

Topschools – This refers to homework or prep. Possibly the most used slang term in the school, used even by the teachers. It derives from when the school was situated in the library and the boys did their homework in a room on the top floor of the school.

Changes – Any activity that requires getting changed for, such as sports.

Eccy leccy – This is a form of detention, where the student is required to do an extra hour of work on a Saturday. It translates as 'extra lesson'.

Festivals

Shrewsbury hosts several festivals, the most notable of all being the **Shrewsbury Flower Show**, the oldest flower show in the world. It began in 1836 as a carnation and gooseberry show. In 1857 the Shropshire Horticultural Society announced that it was staging a flower show in a large marquee, and it has been held every year since. It takes place over two days in mid-August in the Quarry and includes flower displays, fruit and vegetable displays, arts and crafts and music. It also throws a traditional firework display in the evening.

Another popular show is the **Shrewsbury Folk Festival**, which began in 1997 as the Bridgenorth Folk Festival. It takes place over four days around the August Bank Holiday weekend in the West Midlands Showground. It celebrates folk and world music and traditional dance. **Shrewsbury Bookfest** began not long after the folk festival in 1999 and aims to 'inspire, enthuse and entertain children through literature and the arts'. At the time of its conception, it was the only festival of its type in the country. It is an annual festival that takes place around the first May Bank Holiday and won a Queen's Award for Voluntary Service in 2009.

Shrewsbury saw the birth of the **Shrewsbury International Cartoon Festival** in 2003, which attracts amazing cartoonists and caricaturists from around the world. The **Shrewsbury International Street Theatre Festival** was established in 2005, becoming an instant hit with the locals. It takes place on the first weekend of September and if you were to visit at this time you would see the streets full of people juggling, dancing, singing and performing magic tricks.

Shrewsbury continues its solid reputation for creating and throwing fun, family-friendly festivals, and in 2011 the **Shrewsbury Fields Forever** festival was born, attracting some incredible contemporary artists and up-and-coming acts.

Secret Shrewsbury

Shrewsbury is full of interesting, tucked-away pubs, cafés, restaurants and shops that are hidden in the various cobbled shuts and streets. It also contains many hidden gems:

St Chad's pendulum – This well-loved church is home to a 52ft-long pendulum, which is a rarity due to its length. These longer pendulums often suffer from circular error, which affects timekeeping, and for this reason this pendulum is one of the longest of its kind in the world.

Shrewsbury station's carvings – In an attempt to recreate the carvings found on the walls of the Shrewsbury Library, elaborate Tudor-style carvings can be found outside the windows of the Shrewsbury railway station. Each carving is different and worth a viewing.

St Mary's 'Jesse' window – St Mary's is famous for its stained glass. The most notable of the collection is arguably a fourteenth-century depiction of the Tree of Jesse, father of King David. It is located on the east window and portrays various figures from the Old Testament in vibrant, contrasting colours.

Laura's Tower – This is often skipped when visiting Shrewsbury, but the view from Laura's Tower is probably the best in town. From this location you can see for miles, and it is conveniently located a very short walk from the castle.

Drapers Hall – This building dates back to 1556 and is rich with history. Inside the building are beautiful exposed beams, wood panelling and a seventeenth-century fireplace.

St Mary's Shut – This shut is not only the narrowest shut in town, but is one of the smallest in the country. It is sometimes referred to as 'Little Shut' and most of its walls retain their original Tudor style.

Shrewsbury Town FC

Shrewsbury Town FC was created in 1886 and was elected into the Football League in 1950. They are known affectionately as 'Shrews' or the 'Blues', due to the colour of their uniform. Shrewsbury Town FC spent most of their history playing at Gay Meadow, but moved to Greenhous Meadow in 2007.

Shrewsbury Town has provided a number of quality international footballers including Joe Hart, David Edwards, Bernard McNally and Kevin Seabury. It has also attracted a few big names, including Mark Atkins, Nigel Jemson, Ian Woan and Steven 'Oggy' Ogrizovic.

Trivia:

Longest serving player – Dave Walton (seven years)

Top goal-scorer of all time – Arthur 'The Gunner' Rowley (152 league goals)

Most goals in a single season – Arthur 'The Gunner' Rowley (35 goals in 43 games in 1958-1959)

Most appearances – Mickey Brown (418 appearances over his three periods)

Record transfer fees paid – £170,000 for Grant Holt in 2008

Record transfer fees received – £250,000 for David Edwards in 2007

All-time cult hero (as voted by the viewers of *Football Focus*) – Dean Spink

Sports Clubs

Badminton – London Road Badminton Club, London Road

Cricket – Shrewsbury Cricket Club, London Road

Athletics – Shrewsbury Athletic Club, Gains Park

Swimming – Shrewsbury Amateur Swimming Club, Priory Road

Rowing – Pengwern Boat Club, Kingsland

Netball – Shrewsbury Netball Club, Longden Road

Hockey – Shrewsbury Hockey Club, Longden Road

Websites

www.visitshrewsbury.com

www.shrewsburyguide.info

www.shropshiretourism.co.uk

www.virtual-shropshire.co.uk

www.thebestof.co.uk/local/shrewsbury/business-guide/
tourist-attractions

www.attractions.walesdirectory.co.uk/Shrewsbury.htm

www.shrewsburytown.co.uk

www.shrewsburyshopping.co.uk

www.shrewsbury.org.uk

www.stchadschurchshrewsbury.com

www.secretshropshire.org.uk/Content/Learn/Journey/
Shrewsbury.asp

Shrewsbury from the School in 1900

Shrewsbury in 1900

Shrewsbury Now

Future Plans

Shrewsbury has a few changes planned for its town. One such change is the addition of a Premier Inn hotel, which will be built on Smithfield Road in the middle of the town. The hotel, which is scheduled to be opened in 2012, will consist of 127 rooms and will create an extra sixty jobs for the town. When the building was proposed, it was hoped that such a hotel would also bring in business for the retail and tourist industry.

An additional building is proposed for Shrewsbury Sixth Form School, which would cost approximately £1 million and would house the geography, environmental sciences and geology departments. The building would replace the portable classrooms that are being used temporarily. Plans to build have been complicated by a report from Shropshire Council's Archaeology Service, which suggests that there could possibly be medieval human remains underneath the proposed site.

Things to Do Checklist...

The medieval town of Shrewsbury, with a history of more than 1,500 years, is a unique place, with many things to see and do. When you are in town, try to tick everything off the following list:

Visit the Shrewsbury Castle and the Shropshire Regimental Museum ☐

Walk up the pathway from the castle to see the view from Laura's Tower ☐

Take a walk around Shrewsbury Town Public Library and take a photo of the Darwin Statue ☐

Go to St Chad's church and find Scrooge's grave ☐

Have a cup of tea at Poppy's Restaurant and Tudor Tea Rooms ☐

Go next door to Simon Baynes Books and Music and buy an old second-hand book ☐

Go to the Old Market Hall and see a film, if you have the time ☐

Buy a trinket from Wysteria Lane ☐

Take a 40 minute cruise around the River Severn on the *Sabrina* boat ☐

Go to the Quarry for a walk around the grounds and see the flowers. Stop to have a picnic ☐

Go to the Salopian Bar and have a glass of Shropshire Lad ☐

Take a look at the controversial Quantum Leap structure ☐

Captions and Credits

All images are either personal photographs or copyright free, and used with grateful thanks to all the photographers whose pictures I have used.

Page:

59: Sheet music (SXC)

61: Shrewsbury Castle (Samantha Lyon)

63: St Alkmund's church (Samantha Lyon); Shrewsbury Library (Samantha Lyon)

65: St Chad's interior (Samantha Lyon); St Mary's interior (Samantha Lyon)

67: Old Market Hall (Samantha Lyon); Old Market Hall (Samantha Lyon)

69: St Mary's interior (Samantha Lyon); St Mary's exterior (Samantha Lyon)

71: The Dingle 180° (Samantha Lyon)

73: Banded Demoiselle (dixonsej); the Dingle (Samantha Lyon); mallard (Josh Cantrell)

75: Statue of Sabrina (Samantha Lyon); entrance arch (Samantha Lyon)

77: The Loggerheads (Samantha Lyon); Salopian Bar (Samantha Lyon)

79: Wysteria Lane (Samantha Lyon)

81: Welsh Bridge (Samantha Lyon); Welsh Bridge (Samantha Lyon); Kingsland Bridge (Dr Neil Clifton)

83: Baby feet 2 (SXC)

85: Books and pages (SXC)

87: Flood barriers (David Gruar)

89: *Sabrina* tours (Samantha Lyon); *Sabrina* tours (Samantha Lyon)

95: Timber-framed buildings (Samantha Lyon); the Dingle (Samantha Lyon)

97: Film reel (SXC); Shrewsbury Bus Station (Samantha Lyon)

99: Clive of India (Samantha Lyon); St Michael's Statue (Samantha Lyon); Darwin Gate (Samantha Lyon)

100: Old Market Hall (Samantha Lyon)

101: Quantum Leap (Samantha Lyon)

102-103: St Chad's 180° (Samantha Lyon); the Dingle 180° (Samantha Lyon)

105: Laura's Tower (Samantha Lyon); detail on Old Market Hall (Samantha Lyon)

107: Shrewsbury Flower Show (Roy Haworth); Shrewsbury Flower Show activities (Roy Haworth)

109: Wysteria Lane (Samantha Lyon); La Lanterna (Samantha Lyon)

110-111: Simon Baynes Books and Music; graffiti; Darwinian graffiti; more graffiti (all Samantha Lyon)

113: Soccer ball (SXC)

115: Athletics II (SXC); cricket (SXC)

117: Laptop work (SXC)

119: Shrewsbury from the School (LC-DIG-ppmsc-08834)

120-121: Shrewsbury Square then (LC-DIG-ppmsc-08836); Shrewsbury Square now (Samantha Lyon); Old Market Hall then (LC-DIG-ppmsc-08835); Old Market Hall now (Samantha Lyon)

123: The Quarry (Samantha Lyon)

125: Poppy's Tudor Tea Rooms (Samantha Lyon); Wysteria Lane (Samantha Lyon); the Dingle (Samantha Lyon)

128: English Bridge in 1900 (LC-DIG-ppmsc-08837)

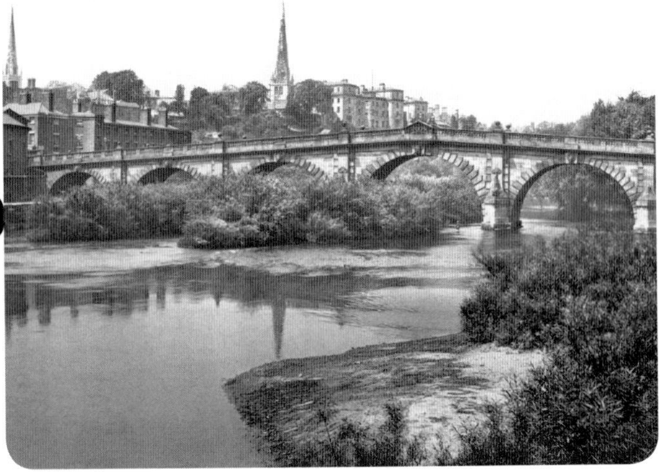